Classic Pop So PLAYALONG! FOR VIOLIN

Ten hit songs in melody line arrangements
by Barrie Carson Turner

Chester Music
8/9 Frith Street London W1D 3JB

This book © Copyright 2001 Chester Music
ISBN 0-7119-8592-8
Order No. CH61832
Music processed by Enigma Music
Cover design by Chloë Alexander
Printed in the United Kingdom

Warning: the photocopying of any pages in this publication is illegal.
If copies are made in breach of copyright the publisher will, where possible, sue for damages.

2 Become 1 28

Angels 23

Candle In The Wind 15

Chiquitita 20

(Everything I Do) I Do It For You 21

Here, There and Everywhere 11

Imagine 26

Never Ever 30

No Matter What 12

Tragedy 18

Practice points

Each book in the *Applause* series includes suggestions – 'practice points' –
on the practice and performance of the pieces in the book.

Each piece has its own list of practice points and exercises to help you in your study of
the music. All the exercises, unless we tell you otherwise, follow a set routine.
The music is first played for you by our soloist, and then you repeat the music a second
and a third time. Metronome clicks introduce each exercise and continue throughout the music,
without a break, for all three repetitions, to help you maintain the beat.
Where helpful, the exercises are slower than the music on the recording.

We hope you will find the practice points useful.

1 Here, There And Everywhere

• Play this gentle song in a relaxed, quiet manner.

Exercise (CD Track 22)

This exercise, bars 20 - 25, includes many accidentals - the consequence of the music changing key.
We are therefore taking this music more slowly than the recording. The music begins with three crotchet clicks.

• Although this song is fairly slow, be careful not to trip over the many tied notes.
• Bars 26 - 31 are a repeat of bars 6 - 11. Knowing where the music repeats saves you practice time.

2 No Matter What

• Play this gentle melody in an easy flowing style.

Exercise (CD Track 23)

This exercise is taken from the opening of the song, bars 9 - 16. The music begins after four crotchet clicks.
Notice each phrase begins with a quaver rest. Listen first as we play, then you repeat the music twice.

• Take care with the change of key in bar 33

- Notice the change of tempo in bars 61 - 63. Play the melody *tenuto* and follow the recording carefully so as to maintain the correct speed. The cymbal will mark out the new slow beat for you. The music returns to the original tempo in bar 64.

3 Candle In The Wind

- This is a fairly relaxed piece which should be played gently and with feeling.

Exercise 1 (CD Track 24)

Exercise 1 is taken from the beginning of the song, bars 5 - 11. The music begins after eight crotchet clicks. Listen first as we play, then you repeat the music twice.

Exercise 2 (CD Track 25)

Exercise 2, bars 20 - 27, is taken from the beginning of the chorus of the song. Take care with the tied notes in the last three bars. The music begins after three crotchet clicks.

- Be sure to count the instrumental bars 35 - 41 carefully.
- Notice that bars 42 - 48 are identical to bars 5 - 11.
- Take care with intonation in this piece - especially the notes B♭, E♭ and A♭. Playing in third position will help you avoid '4th finger back' and improve your intonation.

4 Tragedy

- The verse in this song uses rising sequential phrases to build drama and excitement, which reaches its peak in the chorus. Try and reflect this urgency in your own playing.

Exercise 1 (CD Track 26)

Powerful rhythms are used to stress the urgency of the words of the chorus, particularly on the word 'tragedy'. Exercise 1, bars 33 - 36, introduces you to the opening bars of the chorus. Ensure the rhythms are crisp and accurate. The music is slower than the recording, and begins after four crotchet clicks. Listen first as we play, then you repeat the music twice.

Exercise 2 (CD Track 27)

The music of Exercise 2, bars 37 - 39, follows on from that of Exercise 1. You will see many crotchet triplets here. Play bar 37 first without the tie, if you find the rhythm difficult. It is easier to play crotchet triplets to a minim, rather than a crotchet count. We have therefore used minim beats for the clicks. The music begins after four minim clicks.

- Notice the change of time to 2/4 in bar 30.
- Bars 41 - 47 are a repeat of 33 - 39. Knowing where the music repeats is always useful: it's then possible to avoid practising the same bars twice.
- If you are unsure how to play the syncopated rhythm in bars 53 - 56, listen to the opening bars of the song, where it also appears.

5 Chiquitita

- Although the melody of this song may look difficult, it is not. The rhythms are straightforward, and easy to learn.
- The rhythm which begins the song in bar 2 is worth committing to memory, as it occurs many times during the music.
- Take your lead from the band track, and play this music with energy and bounce.

Exercise 1 (CD Track 28)

Exercise 1 is made up of bars 10 - 17. The music begins after four crotchet clicks, but notice the solo part waits a further beat and a half before it begins. Listen first, then repeat the music twice.

Exercise 2 (CD Track 29)

The music for Exercise 2, bars 18 - 21, includes a change of time for one bar only from 4/4 to the unusual time signature of 5/4. It's important you count these bars carefully. The music begins after four crotchet clicks, but notice the solo part waits a further beat and a half before it begins.

- Notice the 5/4 bar occurs again in bar 28.
- Follow the band track carefully during the *rit.*, which begins in bar 39.

6 (Everything I Do) I Do It For You

- This piece has many tricky rhythms, and much syncopation. Spend some time practising the rhythms you find difficult before you attempt the exercises, or the solo part.
- This is a slow song which should be played gently and with feeling.

Exercise 1 (CD Track 30)

The music of Exercise 1, bars 5 - 12, is taken from the opening of the song. Count the rests carefully. Counting is one of the most important ways to tackle complex rhythms. The music begins with four crotchet clicks. Notice the solo part begins with a crotchet rest.

Exercise 2 (CD Track 31)

Exercise 2, bars 41 - 48, is taken from the close of the song. The solo part begins immediately after the third introductory click. Notice the changes of time to 2/4, then to 4/4, and then back to 2/4 again, finishing in 4/4 at the end of the exercise. Be aware that when you repeat the music, the opening semiquavers follow immediately on from the minim in the last bar. The music begins after three crotchet clicks.

- Follow the band track carefully at the end of the song. Notice the *rall.*, which begins at bar 49.

7 Angels

- As you play this piece, listen to the piano chords on the band track which mark out the crotchet beats. This will help you play the tricky rhythms accurately.

Exercise (CD Track 32)

The music of this exercise comes from the chorus and is rhythmically quite difficult. For this reason we will give you the beat in quaver clicks. Notice that the second phrase of music is a variation of the first. The music begins after three quaver clicks.

- Don't forget to practise the tied note rhythms first without the ties if you find them difficult.
- Pay careful attention to the bowing directions.
- Follow the recording carefully in the penultimate bar in order to pace the *rit.* accurately.

8 Imagine

- Many of the rhythms in this piece are difficult and syncopated. It may help you to think of the words of the song as you play, if you are familiar with the original recording.
- The melody of this song is broken up into many phrases, separated by rests. Make sure you count the rests accurately.

Exercise 1 (CD Track 33)

Exercise 1 concentrates on bars 5 - 8, the opening two phrases of the song. Do you see that these phrases and the two phrases that follow are variations of the same melody?
The music of this exercise is slower than the recording, and we have used quavers as the main beat.
This exercise begins after eight quaver clicks - but notice the solo part begins with a dotted-quaver rest.
Listen first as we play, then you repeat the music twice. There are many rests in this exercise, so you must count the clicks carefully.

Exercise 2 (CD Track 34)

The music for Exercise 2 is taken from the middle section of the song, bars 33 - 36 and is repeated at the end, bars 53 - 56. The rhythms are again demanding, and for this reason we have used the same slow speed of the previous exercise, with quaver clicks to mark the beat. The music begins after eight quaver clicks, but notice the solo part begins with a dotted-quaver rest.

- Practise this song first without the recording, at the speed we use for the exercises, counting in quavers. The best way to learn difficult rhythms is to practise them slowly. When you are sure of the rhythms, gradually increase the tempo, but continue to count.

9 2 Become 1

- This piece uses much syncopation. If you know the words of the song, use these to help you tackle the demanding rhythms.

Exercise (CD Track 35)

This exercise, bars 5 - 8, is taken from the opening of the song. The music begins with four crotchet clicks. But before you begin, spend some time examining the rhythms in the opening two bars of the music. Listen first as we play, then you repeat the music twice.

- There is much in this song that is very similar, if not an exact repetition; so your task of learning the piece is not as formidable as you might initially think.
- Notice that the last three phrases of the music are identical.

10 Never Ever

- Play the opening introductory melody broadly and smoothly.
- You may find it helpful to count this piece in quavers.
- The semiquavers in this piece should be 'gently swung' as directed. Listen to the full performance track first to get into the feel of the music.

Exercise 1 (CD Track 36)

The rhythms are difficult throughout this piece. Exercise 1, bars 17 - 20, demonstrates the type of rhythms you will meet. Listen first as we play, then you repeat the music twice. The music begins after eight quaver clicks.

Exercise 2 (CD Track 37)

The music of Exercise 2, bars 27 - 32, also contains difficult rhythms. Count eight quavers per bar.
Listen first as we play, then you repeat the music twice. The music begins after eight quaver clicks.

- The bowing is tricky in this piece - follow the bowing marks carefully.

Here, There And Everywhere

Words & Music by John Lennon & Paul McCartney

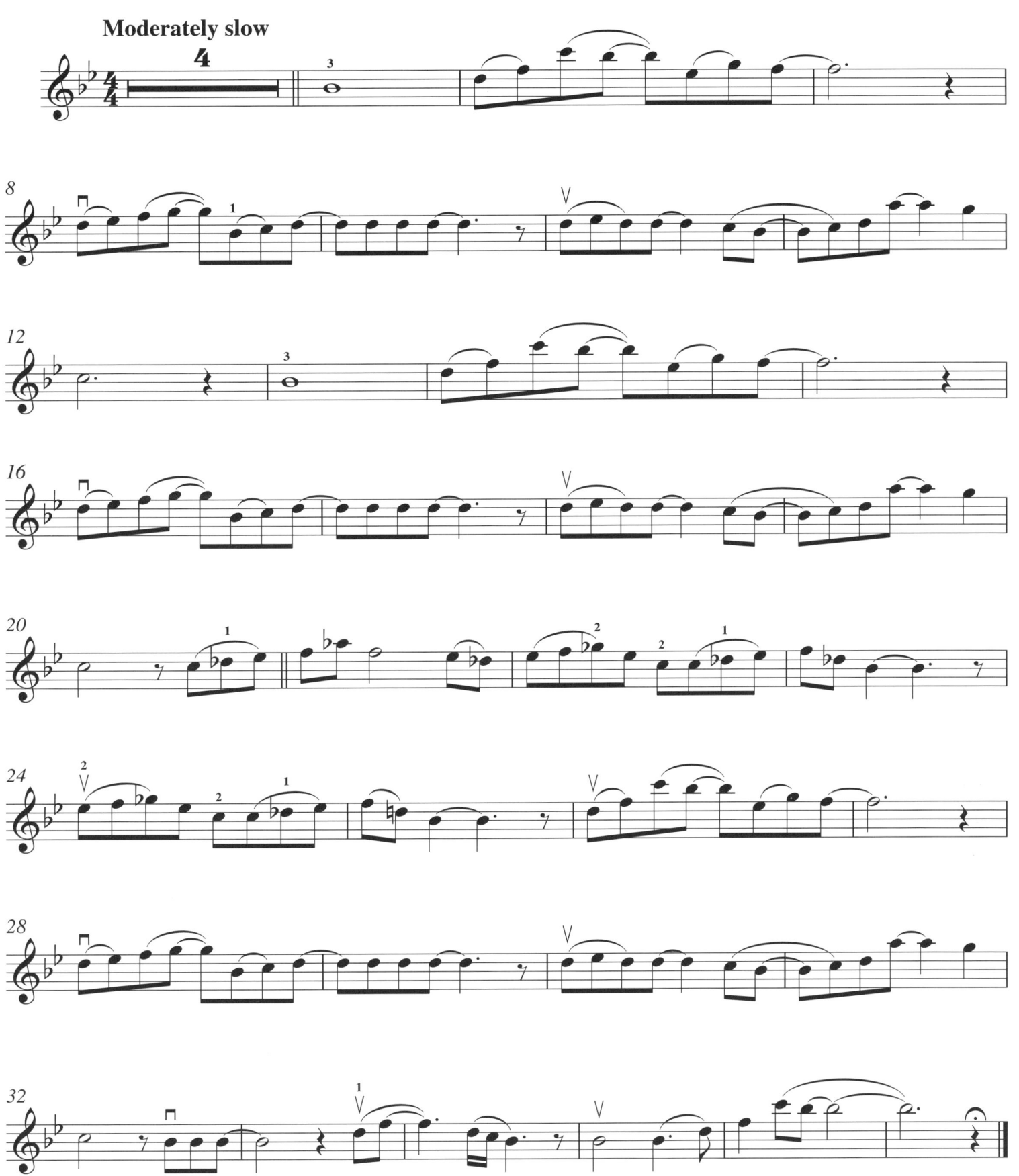

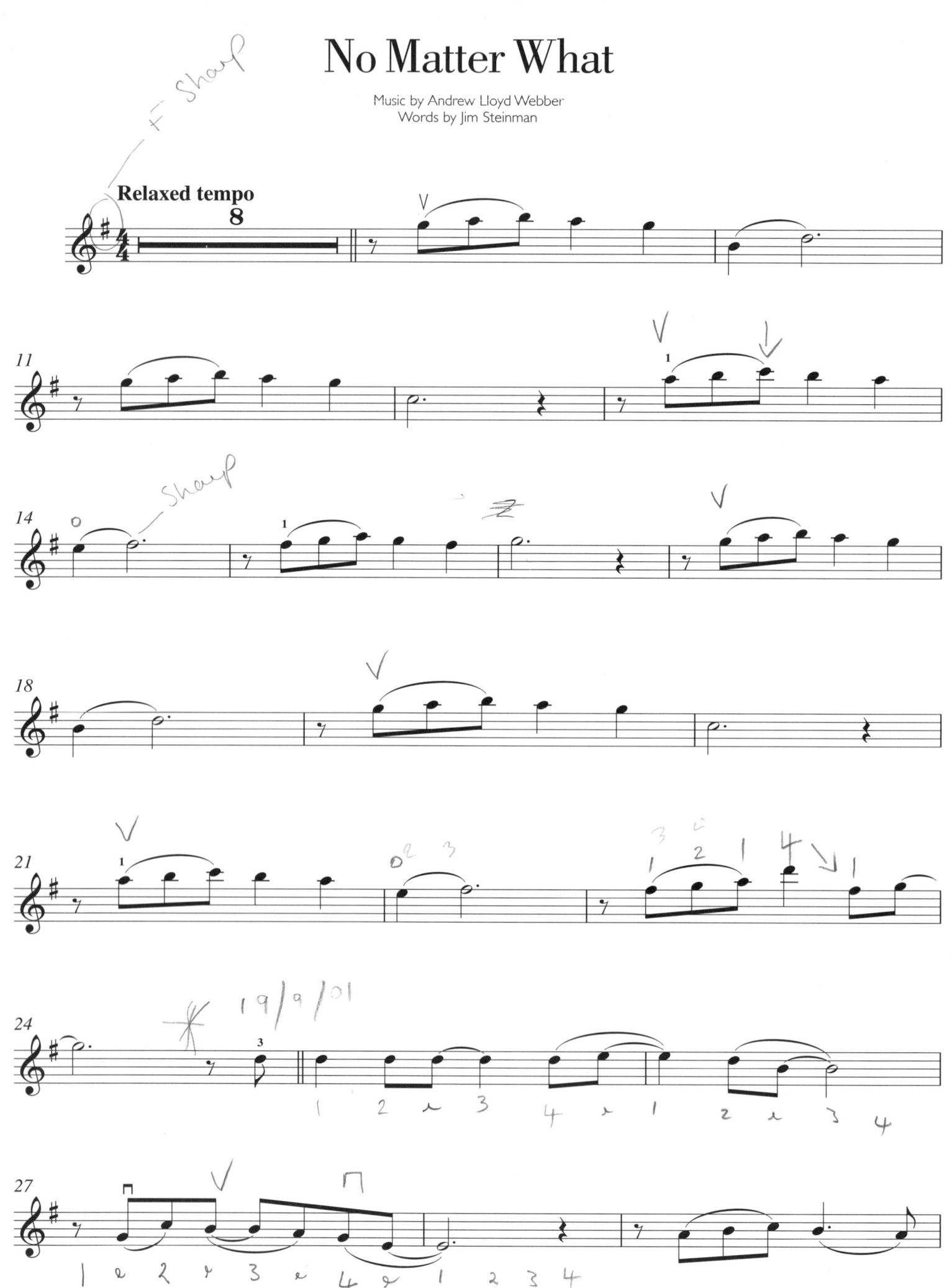

No Matter What

Music by Andrew Lloyd Webber
Words by Jim Steinman

Candle In The Wind

Words & Music by Elton John & Bernie Taupin

Tragedy

Words & Music by Barry Gibb, Maurice Gibb & Robin Gibb

Chiquitita

Words & Music by Benny Andersson & Björn Ulvaeus

(Everything I Do) I Do It For You

Words by Bryan Adams & Robert John Lange
Music by Michael Kamen

Angels

Words & Music by Robbie Williams & Guy Chambers

Imagine
Words & Music by John Lennon

© Copyright 1971 Lenono Music.
All Rights Reserved. International Copyright Secured.

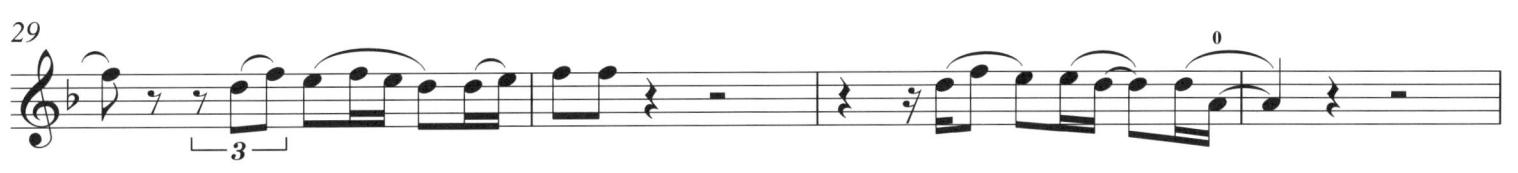
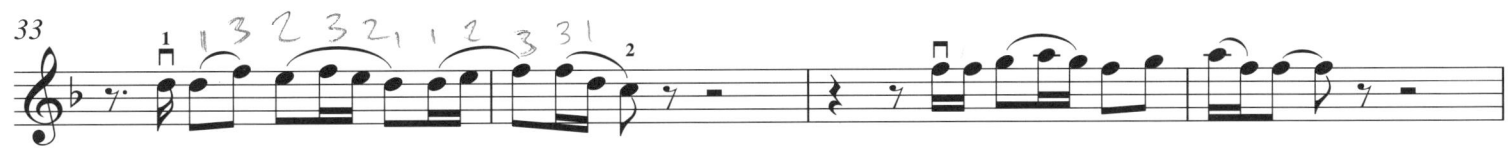

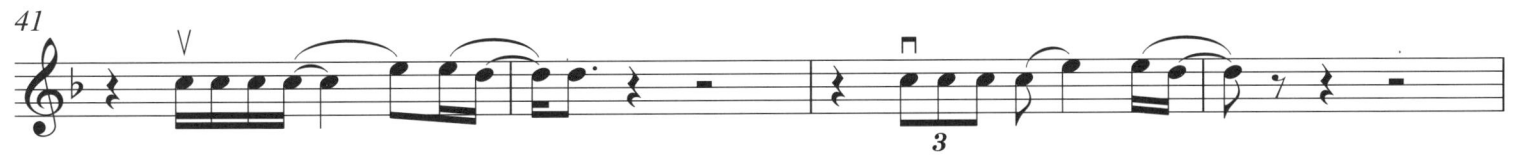

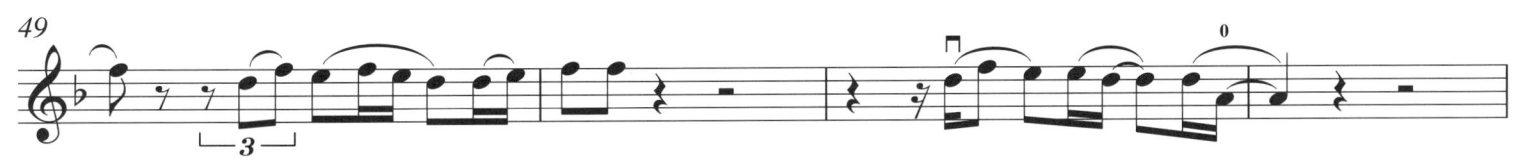

2 Become 1

Words & Music by Victoria Adams, Melanie Brown, Emma Bunton, Melanie Chisholm, Geri Halliwell, Matt Rowe & Richard Stannard

Never Ever

Words & Music by Shaznay Lewis, Esmail Jazayeri & Sean Mather

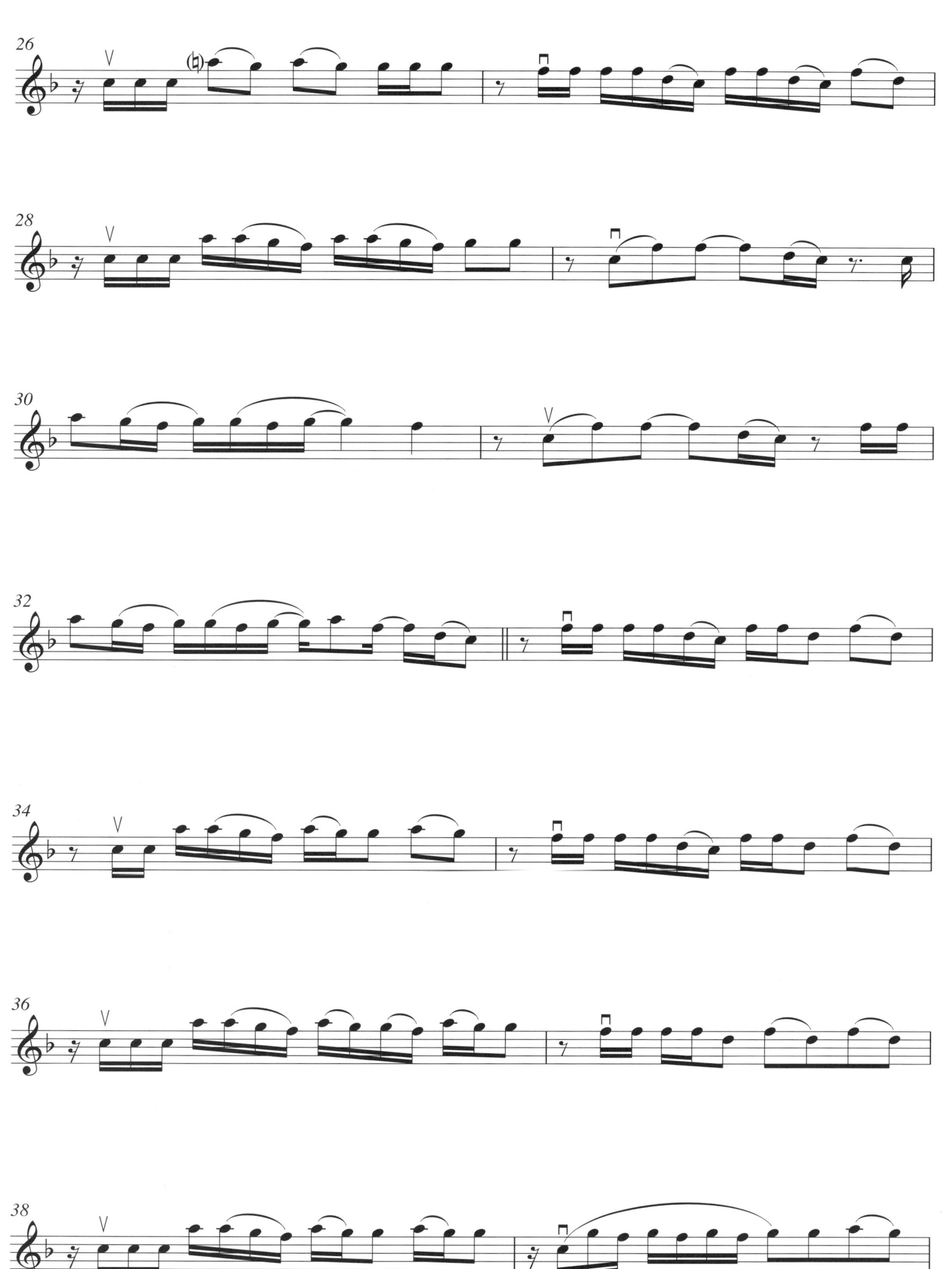

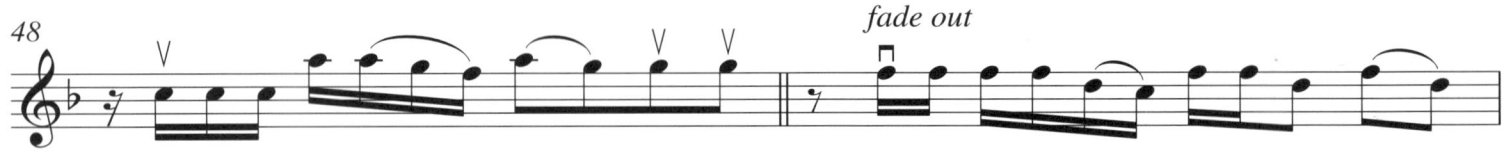